Facts
About

Forests

DONNA BAILEY

STECK-VAUGHN
LIBRARY
Austin, Texas

How to Use This Book

This book tells you many things about forests and trees. There is a Table of Contents on the next page. It shows you what each double page of the book is about. For example, pages 8 and 9 tell you about "Trees with Wide Leaves."

On many of these pages you will find some words that are printed in **bold** type. The bold type shows you that these words are in the Glossary on pages 46 and 47. The Glossary explains the meaning of some words that may be new to you.

At the very end of the book there is an Index. The Index tells you where to find certain words in the book. For example, you can use it to look up words like deciduous, chlorophyll, growth ring, and many other words to do with forests and trees.

Published in the United States in 1990 by Steck-Vaughn Co., Austin, Texas, a subsidiary of National Education Corporation.

© Macmillan Publishers Ltd 1989
Artwork © BLA Publishing Limited 1988

Material used in this book first appeared in Macmillan World Library: Trees and Forests. Published by Macmillan Children's Books

Printed in the United States
1 2 3 4 5 6 7 8 9 0 LB 94 93 92 91 90

Library of Congress Cataloging-in-Publication Data

Bailey, Donna.
    Forests / Donna Bailey.
        p.   cm. — (Facts about)
    "First appeared in Macmillan World library: Trees and forests. Published by Macmillan Children's Books" — T.p. verso.
    Summary: Discusses the types of forests, the trees that constitute them, the clearing and planting of forests, and their interaction with both humans and wildlife.
    ISBN 0–8114–2512–6
    1. Forest ecology — Juvenile literature.   2. Trees— Juvenile literature.   3. Forests and forestry — Juvenile literature.   4. Forest fauna — Juvenile literature.   [1. Forests and forestry.   2. Forest ecology.   3. Ecology.]
I. Title.   II. Series.   89-26106
QK938.F6B33   1990   CIP
574.5'.2642—dc20   AC

Contents

Introduction

Forests used to cover one-third of all the land on Earth.

Many of the forests have been cut down to provide wood or **timber** and to make room for growing different crops. Today much of the cleared land looks like the farmland in the picture.

Some trees produce fruit like bananas
that we can eat.

The woman in the picture is picking
bananas on a **plantation.** She picks
the bananas when they are green
before they are ripe. Then the
bananas will not be too ripe when
they get to our stores.

The Tree

A tree has a single woody stem called a **trunk,** a **crown** of leaves and branches, and roots.

The roots go down into the ground and spread out to keep the tree in place. The roots collect water and **minerals** from the soil. A single tree may take in over 50 gallons of water each day.

The roots turn the water and minerals into a sticky juice called **sap.** The sap rises up the trunk to the leaves, where it is turned into food for the tree.

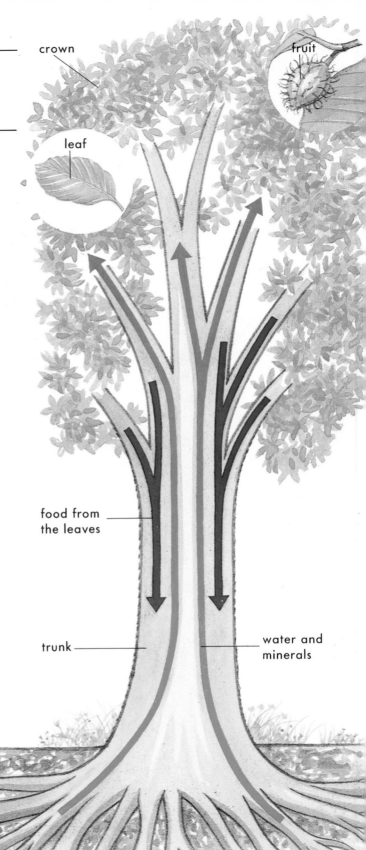

crown

fruit

leaf

food from the leaves

trunk

water and minerals

inside a tree trunk

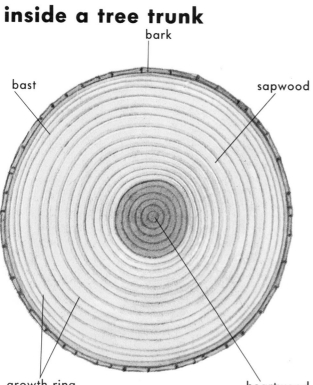

bark

bast

sapwood

growth ring

heartwood

Some trees are very old. The bristlecone pines in North America are the oldest trees in the world. They grow very slowly and have twisted shapes. One of these trees is more than 4,600 years old. It is the oldest living tree in the world.

A tree trunk grows bigger each year by adding a new ring of wood, called a **growth ring.**

The new wood grown in the spring is pale and the new summer wood is dark. If you count all the dark rings or the light wood you can tell how old the tree is.

a bristlecone pine

7

Trees with Wide Leaves

Broad-leaved trees have wide, flat leaves and grow flowers.

The flowers of the Japanese cherry tree are brightly colored.

Broad-leaved trees like teak and oak are called **hardwoods** because their trunks have very hard wood.

cherry

teak

English oak

8

Broad-leaved trees growing in cool areas that lose their leaves before winter are called **deciduous** trees. Their leaves dry up and they change color.

Trees like the holly that keep their leaves all through the year are called **evergreens.**

Broad-leaved trees that grow in hot areas are evergreens, like teak.

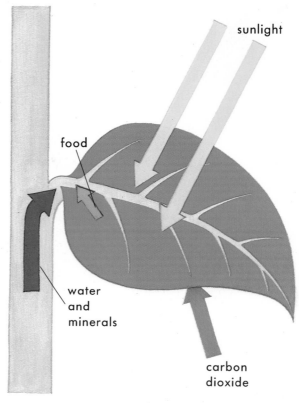

sunlight

food

water and minerals

carbon dioxide

how a leaf makes food

Leaves use the water and minerals from the roots to make food for the tree. They also use sunlight and a gas from the air called **carbon dioxide.**

A green substance in the leaves called **chlorophyll** mixes the water, minerals, gas, and sunlight to make the food.

holly

9

Trees with Cones

Norway spruce

Western red cedar

Trees with cones are called **conifers.** Most have needle-like leaves and are evergreens, like firs, pines, cedars, and spruces.

Conifers grow woody cones instead of flowers, and can live in colder, drier places than broad-leaved trees. They can survive high up in mountains where there is snow and cold winds. Conifers have a pointed shape so that snow can slide off their branches.

Scotch
pine

Douglas
fir

Trees grow well on the lower slopes of mountains. No trees can grow near the **summit** above the tree line.

tree line

If you climb a mountain, you will see that the types of tree change as you climb higher. Lower down, a mixture of trees grow. Farther up, it is colder and the soil is poor. Only the toughest conifers can survive the dry, cold conditions.

Palms and Ferns

The trunk of a palm tree does not grow branches. It grows straight upward like a giant stalk, so it does not make growth rings. Inside the trunk are bunches of woody tubes that carry water up to the leaves.

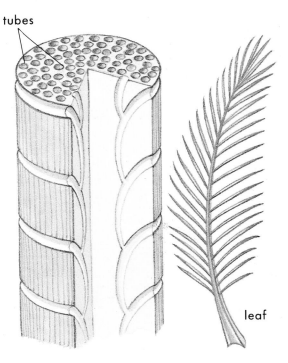

tubes

leaf

inside the trunk of a palm tree

A palm tree grows a bunch of big leaves from the top of the trunk. The leaves are split into spiky strips that let the wind through. We eat the fruits of palm trees such as coconut palms and date palms.

Tree ferns are like palm trees but they do not grow fruits and seeds.

a tree fern

How Trees Begin

A tree in flower produces fruit and seeds. A tiny number of these seeds will grow into new trees.

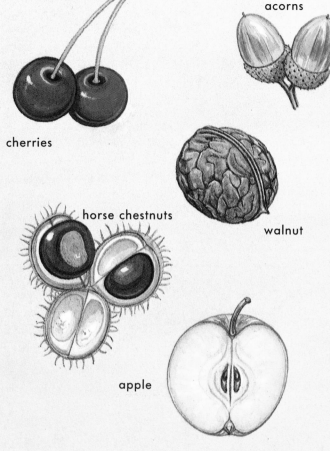

cherries

acorns

horse chestnuts

walnut

apple

tree in flower

Each kind of tree has its own special fruit and seed. Fruit we eat, like apples or cherries, are soft fruit. Trees like a walnut or oak have hard fruits, or nuts. Horse chestnuts have a spiky covering over their fruit to stop hungry animals from eating them.

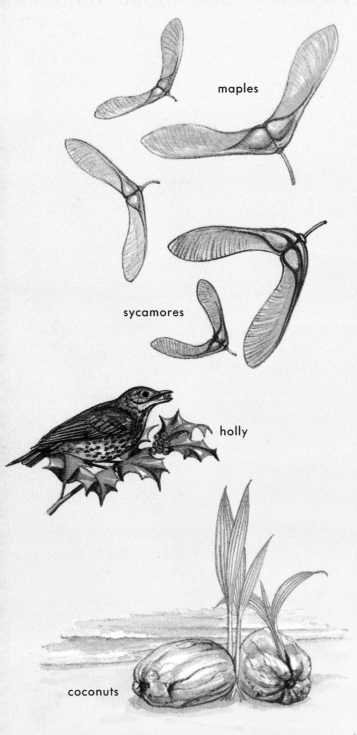

maples

sycamores

holly

coconuts

**seeds that drop on
areas of good soil
grow into seedlings**

The seeds leave the trees
in different ways.
Some seeds have wings and
are blown by the wind.
   Birds eat the berries of
trees such as holly.
The seeds of the berries
are spread by the birds
in their droppings.
   Some seeds like palm
tree seeds float across
the sea to beaches where
they grow into new palms.
   The seed grows roots, a
stem, and leaves to make
the **seedling** of a new tree.

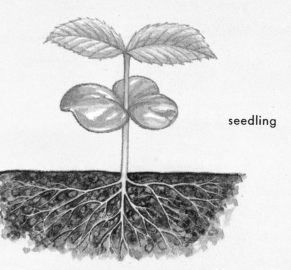

seedling

15

Types of Forest

canopy

buttress

Tropical forests have a warm wet climate, and plants grow well there. Trees in a tropical forest grow close together and their crowns touch one another to make a thick **canopy.** The tallest trees grow to about 230 feet high and push their way through the canopy toward the sun.

a temperate forest

Temperate forests have warm summers and cool winters.
The tallest trees are about 100 feet high.
Young trees take root and struggle for light.
They will never grow well unless an old tree dies and leaves a space with enough light.

Northern forests have short summers and long, cold winters.
The coniferous trees grow close together.
Their branches may die and fall off because they cannot get enough light.
Few plants grow in the ground under the trees.

a coniferous forest

17

Animals in Pine Forests

Different animals live in different kinds of places or **habitats.**

Birds in northern pine forests eat the seeds inside the woody cones. The crossbill in our picture has a specially shaped beak that is crossed at the tip. The crossbill twists the seeds out of the cone.

The birds also eat the insects, beetles, and wasps that live in the forests during the summer.

Other animals, like red squirrels and mice, feed on seeds and insects. Larger animals, like deer and beaver, eat grass, bark, leaves, and twigs.

a red squirrel

Some animals are hunters and kill other animals.

Pine martens climb up the pine trees and catch small birds to eat. Pine martens are rare in Europe now because people hunted them for their fur.

Animals in Woodlands

The temperate woodlands are full of
insects like ants, beetles, and
moths in spring and summer.
The insects attract some birds,
while other birds eat the young
leaves and fruit of the trees.
The largest animals are the deer
which nibble the leaves and twigs.

woodlands in winter

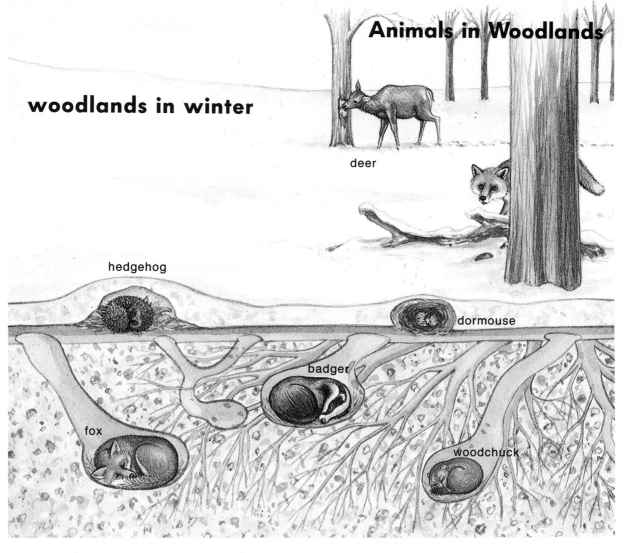

deer

hedgehog

dormouse

badger

fox

woodchuck

In the winter the woodland floor is buried under a layer of snow. Many birds **migrate** to warmer lands.

Dormice and hedgehogs sleep all winter in their nests, and woodchuck **hibernate** in underground burrows. Foxes dig burrows too, and only come out in winter to look for food. Deer nibble the bark of the trees.

21

Animals in Rain Forests

There is always a lot of food for
animals in tropical rain forests.
Many of the animals live in the
trees, like this spider monkey, which
grips the branches with its tail.
The sloth also climbs well and
often hangs upside down on a branch.
There are also lots of butterflies,
beetles, and snakes in the trees.

flying snake

spider
monkey

sloth

birdwing
butterfly

22

**great
hornbills**

chameleon

hercules beetle

The trees are full of
brightly colored birds
which move together in
flocks to find food.

The great hornbill feeds
on fruit, but many birds
look for small animals,
like chameleons, to eat.

Chameleons hide among
the leaves and can change
the color of their skin.

23

Where Are the Forests?

The map shows the main forest areas in the world.

Tropical forests have over 100 inches of rain each year and the temperature is always about 75° F.

Warm temperate forests have between 20 and 60 inches of rain each year and the winter temperature rarely drops below 32° F.

Cool temperate forests have between 30 and 60 inches of rain each year. The temperature varies from 5° F in winter to 68° F in summer.

Northern forests have only about 8 inches of rain. The temperature varies from -40° F in winter to 50° F in summer.

The chart shows the names of different kinds of broad-leaved and coniferous trees that grow in different areas of the world.

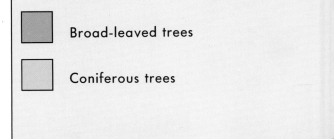

Broad-leaved trees

Coniferous trees

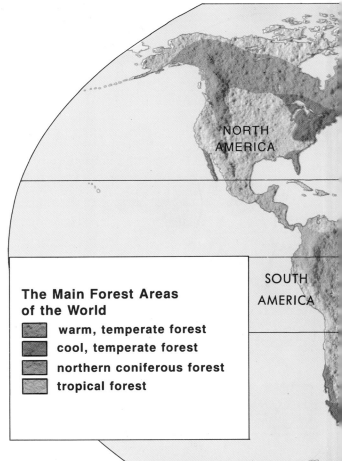

NORTH AMERICA

SOUTH AMERICA

The Main Forest Areas of the World
warm, temperate forest
cool, temperate forest
northern coniferous forest
tropical forest

North America	Alder, Ash, Basswood, Beech, Birch, Cherry, Dogwood, Elm, Gum, Hickory, Hornbeam, Maple, Oak, Plane, Poplar, Sycamore, Walnut, Willow	Cedar, Cypress, Douglas fir, Hemlock, Larch, Pine, Sequoia, Spruce, True fir
South America	Acapu, Balsa, Boxwood, Brazilwood, Greenheart, Hevea, Kingwood, Louro, Mahogany, Peroba, Rosewood, Sajo, Snakewood, Ulmo, Walnut	Alerce, Chile pine, Manio, Parana pine
Europe	Alder, Ash, Beech, Birch, Cherry, Chestnut, Elm, Holly, Oak, Pear, Plane, Poplar, Sycamore, Walnut Willow	Cedar, Cypress, Douglas fir, Larch, Pine, Spruce, Wellingtonia, Yew
Africa	Acacia, Boabab, Boxwood, Ebony, Iroko, Mahogany, Obeche, Odoko, Oil palm, Opepe, Pillarwood, Satinwood, Teak, Utile, Walnut, Wenge	Cedar, Cypress, Pine, Podo, Thuya
Asia	Acacia, Anan, Blackwood, Boxwood, Cinnamon, Gum, Hevea, Kokko, Marblewood, Medang, Meranti, Rosewood, Sandalwood, Teak, Tulipwood, Walnut	Cedar, Chir, Cypress, Juniper, Pine, Spruce
Australia	Ash, Beech, Birch, Blackwood, Brush box, Coachwood, Eucalyptus, Ironbark, Jarrah, Karri, Oak, Peppermint, Stringbark, Tallowwood, Walnut	Kauri, Pine, Rimu

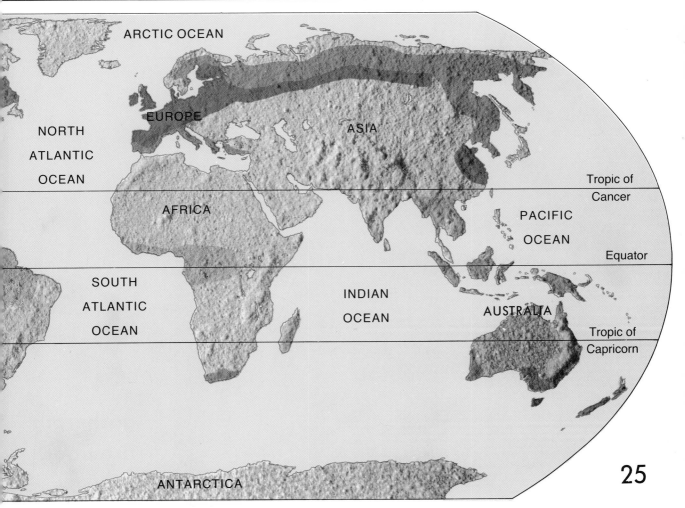

Using the Forests

About half the trees cut down each year are used as firewood for heating and cooking.

We also use timber in buildings, for making doors, floors, window frames, and stairs.

Tables, chairs, and other kinds of furniture can all be made from wood. Some trees give us **resin,** gum, cork, and **latex** from which rubber is made.

gathering firewood

unloading logs from a ship in Finland

Most of these products come from trees growing in many different countries. The people living there sell the products to other countries that need them. Ships load up the timber at the docks to take the wood to another country.

how many things made from wood can you see in this room?

Forests of Europe

Large areas of Europe were once
covered with broad-leaved forests.
Then many of the trees were cleared
to make farmlands to grow crops.

The forests that remained were owned
by rich people who hunted in them.

Trees were cut down to build ships.
It could take 700 oak trees to build
a large warship. Soon all the trees
began to disappear.

People began to realize that unless they planted new trees, the forests would disappear forever.

The forester in our picture is **coppicing** to make poles for a fence.

a warship made from the wood of the oak

Forests of North America

The biggest trees in the world grow in the warmth of California, on the west coast of the United States. These are the massive redwoods and sequoias shown in our picture, which can grow 360 feet tall. The Douglas fir is another giant tree reaching 260 feet.

collecting maple sap

The United States and Canada sell a lot of their timber to other countries. The trees are cut down by **lumberjacks** using powerful saws that can also strip the branches off. Then the logs are tied together in log rafts and floated down the rivers to the sawmills, where they are cut up into planks.

North America has many other trees that have special uses.

Our picture shows the sweet sap being collected from cuts made in the bark of a maple tree. Tubes are put into the tree and the sap runs into a collecting bucket. The sap that is collected is used to make maple syrup and sugar.

timber tied in rafts

Forests of South America

The largest tropical rain forest in the world is in the basin of the Amazon River in South America. The climate is hot and damp and the forest is a thick mass of trees.

There are thousands of different kinds of trees growing there, but most of the forest is wild and there are hardly any roads, so only a few trees can be used for timber.

the Amazon River

on the riverbank

The easiest way to move people and goods through the forest is by river, so the riverbanks are a popular meeting place.

Deep inside the forest groups of South American Indians live in the same way that they have lived for hundreds of years. They hunt and gather fruit and nuts to eat.

33

The main type of forest in Africa is
the tropical rain forest of West Africa
where hardwood trees like teak and
mahogany grow. Huge machines pull these
trees out of the ground and drag
them to the road.

   Now there are not many of these
trees left, so people have planted
other trees like the obeche that
grow more quickly than hardwoods.

Groups of people called pygmies live in the wild forests of Zaire.

Pygmies are the smallest people in the world. Pygmy men are only about 4.9 feet tall. They still follow their old way of life.

Many kinds of fruit trees grow in Africa, including cocoa, coffee, bananas, and **citrus fruits.**

picking coffee

pygmies at home

35

Forests of Asia

The giant trees in the large tropical
forests in the south of Asia have
thick **buttress roots** which start
spreading out well above the ground.
They stop the trees from falling over.

Many rubber trees grow in Malaysia.
A rubber tapper uses a special knife
to cut the bark so the latex runs out.
It is caught in a collecting cup.

a rubber tapper

Thick bamboo forests grow
in the mountains of China.
Bamboo has a tough, hollow
stem and is useful for
building houses and making
bridges or furniture.
The picture shows bamboo
poles being used for
building **scaffolding.**

bamboo scaffolding

Forests of Australia

Most of the trees in Australian forests are eucalyptus trees.
They are evergreens and have a hard wood which is used for building.
Some kinds grow to over 330 feet high.

eucalyptus trees

in the rain forests of Papua New Guinea

Papua New Guinea is a land of mountains and thick rain forests. There are very few roads and the people that live in the mountains have not changed their way of life for hundreds of years.

They build their houses of palm leaves and bamboo from the forest. They grow their own food such as yams, bananas, and sweet potatoes.

39

Forests in Danger

Forests can be destroyed very quickly by fire, wind, or floods.

Many people forget that fires start easily when the ground is dry. A lighted match or a spark can set a whole forest on fire, which may burn for days, killing hundreds of trees.

Strong winds blow down old or rotten trees and tear off branches.

a dead elm tree

Animals can harm a forest.
Insects strip off the
leaves, or burrow into the
bark of trees.
The bark beetle spreads a
disease that destroyed
many elm trees in Europe.
Beavers cut down trees
to build their homes.
Elephants push down whole
trees to eat the leaves,
branches, and soft sapwood.

**a hungry
elephant**

41

The Threat from People

When people cut down trees for fuel, they forget how long trees take to grow. Our picture shows mountains by the coast of Yugoslavia that were once covered with forests.

When the trees are gone there are no roots to hold the soil in place. This can cause **erosion**. The soil is washed away by rain or blown away by wind.

factories

power stations

cars, trucks, and buses

waste gases

chemicals mixing with the air

Many of the forests that are left are in danger from **acid rain.**

Fuel is burned in factories and power stations and the waste gases and **chemicals** pour out of their chimneys. These mix with the air and return to earth in rain, mist, and dust.

chemicals returning to the earth

acid rain kills the leaves on the trees

Forests of the Future

It is likely that there will be more coniferous forests in the future than broad-leaved forests because conifers grow faster, and make good timber. These young pine trees being planted in Brazil will make a thick pine forest in about 30 years.

Countries now are interested in **conservation** and take more care of their forests and trees.

People now replace dead trees, or replant uprooted trees.

Some forests have been made into national parks that have saved some animals and plants from dying out.

Glossary

acid rain rainwater that contains substances that will harm plants, trees, lakes, and buildings.

broad-leaved trees trees that have wide, flat leaves and that grow flowers.

buttress roots roots that give trees support or strength.

canopy the upper layer or roof of branches over a forest.

carbon dioxide one of the gases in the air. Plants breathe in carbon dioxide during the day.

chemicals substances that can change when mixed with others to make a different substance.

chlorophyll the substance that makes leaves green.

citrus fruits lemons, oranges, grapefruits, and similar juicy fruits.

conifers trees that grow cones instead of flowers.

conservation the protection and careful treatment of the countryside, plants, and animals.

coppicing cutting a tree near the ground so that it grows straight, new shoots from its base.

crown the part of the tree above the trunk. The crown is made up of branches, twigs, and leaves.

deciduous a tree that loses its leaves in the winter and grows new ones in the spring.

erosion the wearing away of land by water, wind, and ice.

evergreens trees and bushes that have leaves all year.

growth ring one of the rings that can be seen when a tree or log is cut across the middle.

habitats the places where different animals usually live.

hardwoods strong heavy woods.

hibernate to go to sleep during the cold winter months.

latex a thick, milky liquid that comes from a rubber tree.

lumberjacks people who cut down trees.

migrate to travel long distances to find food or to escape the cold weather.

minerals natural substances found in the ground that have not been formed from plant or animal life.

plantation a large area of land where one type of plant or tree is grown.

resin a sticky liquid that comes from cuts that are made in some trees.

sap the liquid that flows through a plant carrying food and water to the living parts of the plant.

scaffolding materials bound together to make platforms for builders to reach higher parts of buildings.

seedling a very young plant grown from a seed.

summit the top of a mountain.

temperate a type of weather pattern that has mild summers and cool winters. The weather is never very hot, nor very cold.

timber wood that is used for building houses or making things such as furniture.

tropical something to do with or coming from the tropics, which are the hot, damp parts of the world found near the Equator.

trunk the main thick, wooden part of a tree between the roots and the branches.

Index

Acknowledgments
The Publishers wish to thank The Canadian High
Commission for their invaluable assistance in the preparation
of this book.
Photographic credits
(t=top b=bottom l=left r=right)
Cover photograph:
4 Douglas Dickens; 5 ZEFA; 7, 12 Brian Hawkes/NHPA; 13 Alex
Williams/Seaphot; 18 Philip Wayre/NHPA; 19t Claudio
Galasso/Seaphot; 19b R. Balharry/NHPA; 20 Ed Rotberg; 23
Ivan Polunin/NHPA; 26, 27 The Hutchison Library; 28
Ashmolean Museum, Oxford; 29 Ardea; 30 Heather Angel;
30/31 Canadian High Commission; 31 Ardea; 32 South
American Pictures; 33t, 33b, 34, 35t, 35b The Hutchison
Library; 36, 37t Douglas Dickens; 37b, Dennis
Firminger/Seaphot; 38 ZEFA; 39 The Hutchison Library; 40 Peter
Scoones/Seaphot; 41t John Lythgoe/Seaphot; 41b Ernest
Neal/Seaphot; 42/43 ZEFA; 44 Susan Griggs Agency; 45
Forestry Commission